Online Dating For Women

Secret Tips To Online Dating And Finding The Love Of Your Life

By Alexandra Summers

Table of Contents

CHAPTER 1: INTRODUCTION

Love...A simple, four letter word with the utmost complex meaning. Each and every one of us has the desire to be loved and have the need for romance. It's a natural part of our existence - everyone needs love.

However, with all the work, hassles and distractions we experience day to day, not all of us have the leisure time to find that one individual, or someone to fall in love with.

Let's face it, not everyone has the time to linger at night clubs and bars every single week. Not only does clubbing and bars take up a lot of your time, it's also draining, physically and financially.

Of course, there are many other options to meet a man you might like...Speed dating, dating agencies, newspaper columns, coffee houses, phone dating and, of course, online dating.

This guide will help you focus on the simplest, least expensive and most convenient ways to get to know as many quality men as you like...all from the comfort of your own home!

This guide will assist you find a good man, a gentleman, who will love you for the rest of your life. This guide is for women who are looking for a lasting, long-term relationship, not a one night stand or simply casual sex – which is actually not that hard to get for any independent woman.

Ok, now that we got that out of the way, let's focus a little on exactly what this guide is all about: **Online Dating**.

Unlike conventional dating, online dating is not expensive, safe and totally comfortable. You don't need to spend thousands on clothing, dinners and nights out, don't need to spend time with anyone you don't like and can pick, choose and get to know as many men as you like from the comfort of your own home.

On a regular date, you get to meet and spend time with just one man. In the online dating world, you can literally chat and get to know 100 men before you even meet them in person.

You can sit around in your robe, while eating popcorn and still meet the man of your dreams. You can get to know men that interest you and you only need to actually meet a man face-to-face when you are absolutely sure you would like to get to know him better.

According to experts on dating, the principles to conscious dating are:

❖ Realize who you are and what you want by having a clear vision of what life means/holds for you.

❖ Set and achieve a "goal" by developing a workable relationship plan.

❖ Be selective and prepared to take the onus for the choices you make.

❖ Try and attain a balance between the heart and mind--emotions and sensibility.

❖ Use the "law of attraction" to your benefit.

❖ Hone your relationship skills and knowledge.

❖ Make use of well meaning support by creating a support group around you.

❖ Win by being assertive, realistic, and honest—say "no" firmly and when you decide "yes" then stick by your decision. Set down boundaries for yourself—keeps the going clear and focused.

❖ Be a successful and fulfilled single –never put life on hold or make finding a relationship/man the sole purpose of your life.

What Are the Main Advantages of Online Dating?

You never have to meet anyone in person during an online encounter...which can help you avoid shyness and feeling uncomfortable. You can be as sexy, funny and weird as you want to be without actually getting embarrassed (same goes for the men you'll be chatting with).

Also, you choose the type of guy you want to talk to, or meet with. You can simply set your standards and find a man that meets them instead of just taking a stab in the dark.

Instead of hoping that we will bump into the perfect man on the street, or get hooked up with the man of our dreams. We can stop dreaming, take action and simply use online dating as a tool to find the perfect guy (or close to perfect) for ourselves. I know this does not sound as romantic as some of the other options, but it is simply the most realistic one.

The overwhelming success of online dating sites is proof that the "realistic" choice is a lot more effective than simply waiting for Mr. Right. And the fact that dating sites are helping millions of people find true love and romance is proof that just because Online Dating is not something most people fantasize and read about in novels, it is the new, more realistic way to meet the man of your dreams.

So, if you are "old fashioned" I suggest you get caught up with the new times.

According to experts, dating sites have become the "good fairy" of the modern world. They are helping millions of men and women find fruitful relationships. It is using sophisticated technology to further romance.

All you need to know is what you want: long term relationship, friendship, fun and excitement etc. Whatever it is you want; chances are there are dating sites that fit your needs.

So, if you know what you want and are anxious to "get out there" from the comfort of your own home, let's get started!

CHAPTER 2: ONLINE DATING FOR INDEPENDENT WOMEN

Online dating lends time flexibility and a various degree of secrecy…It's really up to you how much or how little you attempt to locate "Mr. Right". You can proceed to learn more about the individual or you can cut the relationship short and move on with no emotional strings attached. The cyber dating world, like the real world, is made up of all kinds of unique individuals – serious, funny, kinky, eccentric, as well as dangerous…

It is important to approach online dating like a pro---a management professional. The Internet is full of opportunities to find a soul mate but one must do it intelligently and with great care.

Modern technology coupled with dating innovations will help you customize your search for the "ideal" man of your dreams. You will be able to sift through thousands of eligible men to find one that matches your needs. A study in the UK revealed that there was a success rate of approximately 94%. Believe it or not there are more than 700+ online dating sites on the Internet and it is a growing business.

As women and men become more computer savvy, socializing on the net is gaining popularity. Matchmaking on the net is today becoming innovative with videos, live voice, instant messaging, and so on.

The wonderful world of online dating allows you to:

❖ Read all about a person and his likes and dislikes in a profile—one does not have to meet the man time and again to glean a small bit of insight into him.

❖ Specify clearly what you are seeking.

❖ Matchmaking services will help you narrow down a choice by using compatibility rankings and questionnaires.

❖ The online service will mail you each day many "possible" profiles for consideration. To be 'efficient' in your quest you would need to write down criteria of your concept of Mr. Right.

❖ Commonly used search options are: profession, location, age, height, physical characteristics, lifestyle, birth sign, and hobbies.

Don't be afraid, online dating is a stress free method of meeting people for fun, friendship, and love. You are the one to decide what kind of relationship you are seeking—a temporary one or a long term one; whether you want commitment or just a casual relationship.

Set your own limits or boundaries and keep to them—decide no sex until I known the man well and follow the dictum. Because a man is dashing and drop dead handsome and has charmed the 'boots off you," don't jump into bed with him—wait until you are sure that's what you want.

By using your computer with the click of your mouse you can explore a world of opportunities. Just 10 minutes on any search engine ---Yahoo, Google, or Alta Vista –and you will have access to:

❖ Dating sites.

❖ Articles discussing different concerns that plague all of us—from makeovers, to what so say, to dating ideas, coping with rejection and so on.

❖ Plenty of advice, tips, as well as "ask a question" sites.

At first, online dating may seem gigantic or intimidating. There are so many choices – the question that will crowd your mind is...

"Which one should I choose?"

First create a budget and decide how much you want to invest on online dating. Some sites charge a one-time fee while others a recurring monthly fee. A few are free. Second, do some research and find out whether anyone known to you has used a site and what their experience was. Third, read an online dating guide —most of these provide valuable information. Then, set aside quality time to 'check out" sites thrown up by search engines...do a personal survey of what each offers.

There are special "niche sites" catering to specific requirements like religious affiliations, sexual preferences, political beliefs and so on. So, if you do have any preferences that you are particular about you must look for sites that offer such choices.

Jot down the pros and cons of a few sites that you are inclined towards and check out the number of members, as well as any reviews by outside agencies on the site in question.

Some sites offer a free, limited period membership—to give you a taste – avail of the offer. Also, consider joining more than one site—it will increase greatly your chances of meeting someone.

Choosing a site is a personal preference. Each site has its advantages as well as disadvantages. Many have several safety measures in place. Yet others are lax and could be misused by members who are not suitable. You need to decide what you're comfortable with.

Most sites will require the creation of a profile that possible dates will read and contact you by. Some sites require a detailed profile while others let you create your own version.

How much you want to reveal --- what aspect of your life/personality, is for you to decide. Keep in mind, what you say should paint a word picture of who you are—be precise as well as honest about yourself.

What the profile does not indicate can be conveyed in subsequent e-mails and chat room chats or over a phone. Don't come on too strongly – men will steer clear of you if they get the impression that you are a strong woman.

If the dating site has specific questions in key areas, like children, try and be totally honest. If you have children, say so. If you want children, say so. You can't build a life-long relationship by misleading a man about something as important as whether you have or would like children.

Remember, *it's a numbers game.* You need to get as many potential lovers to see your profile as possible (within your budget). You also need to be able to review as many profiles as possible.

Don't assume that submitting your profile and attaching a photo is enough. You need to cast your net as wide as possible. Start searching using your desired criteria in your local area and then systematically expand your search until, if necessary, you've covered the whole country – love knows no boundaries. Obviously, it may not be practical for one or both of you to travel several hours to see each other, but don't be too quick to rule this out. Absence can often make the heart grow fonder.

Be sure to look for a site that offers   personality and compatibility testing or advice services. The process in these sites is a bit slower but the ultimate goals reached are what you could be seeking—the chances of your finding the true love of your life are highly likely.

Popular sites are: eharmony.com; match.com; date.com; and americansingles.com. Many daters increase their chances of meeting Mr. Right by joining more than one site.

Do check what safety measures the sites have in place—the most important ones are: anonymous e-mailing, and a secure phone system.

Other must haves are—online instant messaging, photo personals with password protection, voice chat, and local dating advice/activities.

Privacy protection is what most online dating sites aim for. All efforts are made to ensure safety to users:

❖ Most sites have an e-mail system that never reveals a users identity. The system is designed to protect the user's privacy.

- A user name is used that has no connection whatsoever to your e-mail address. The username is coined by the user/member themselves and is a random nomenclature.

- There are blocking options, which can be used to block a person from accessing your profile or even contacting you.

- Many sites have a certification of trust –they are a member of the TRUSTe program. This means that they adhere in every way to established privacy rules.

- Sites also have a BBB online reliability seal, which means the site can be trusted.

Remember, you're in a competition. The more effort you put in, the better the results you'll get.

- It requires very few resources. All that is needed is for you to make your self-available and get in touch with "like minded" singles. The dating site can be accessed from anywhere and by anyone.

- Offers freedom, flexibility, and choice. You make the decision of contacting interesting profiles. You decide whether or not to answer an e-mail or message.

- Posting a profile allows you to limit your search. And listing of criteria in a partner narrows down the search. A search can be tailored to suit—location, physique, age or profession.

- ❖ You can have the freedom to search whenever you like—early morning, late at night, weekends, and so on. Online dating does not set borders of time or location. You need not leave your Pc and find Mr. Right.

- ❖ There are many ways to interact with interesting people. Options include: e-mail, creative icons, chat rooms, instant messaging, games, voice/video greeting, dating meets as well as safe phone calls.

- ❖ You can be in touch with more than one Mr. Possible. There are no restrictions you may be in touch with 5, 20, or even 100.

- ❖ Fears, shyness, inhibitions, and other problems are eased in online dating, as there is no face-to-face contact until you choose to. Embarrassment at being candid or honest is also reduced.

- ❖ Choose an online site with few limitations—one that features domestic as well as international people. Don't limit your options to your immediate neighborhood or town.

- ❖ Read and understand the company's policy page as well as purpose. Be sure to read or ask for their privacy policy. Look up reviews of the site by impartial experts or users. Read the FAQ section thoroughly.

- ❖ Download Alexa Toolbar, which ranks online sites with no.1 being the most popular.

- ❖ Check about the payment system and whether it is secure.

- ❖ Find out and ascertain what security features are in place to protect you from harm.

Quick Tips:

- ❖ Be open about yourself.

- ❖ Use instant messaging as well as "chat rooms" to get to know men better. It is more interactive that e-mails.

- ❖ Once you are certain you would like to get to know a man better use the phone—voices reveal more than typed words. Speak on the phone as often as needed.

- ❖ When you do decide to meet do so in a public place.

- ❖ Always keep safety in mind.

Chapter 3: Avoiding Online Dating Blunders

Most people mistake online dating as simply, click and date...The truth is, online dating is much more than just clicking and meeting an individual who's profile looks too good to be true.

Many women try online dating for a practical joke...they are not serious, when they try it out; the effort made is half measures at best. The key is to make a full fledged effort to succeed.

Another online blunder is thinking men will approach you is wrong. Your "Mr. Right" is not going to come out of thin air. You need to make an effort to contact the type of man that meets your ideal. Read profiles and narrow down candidates that fit your vision of the "right man". Be bold and contact men – don't wait like a wall flower.

Make sure to communicate well - writing one liner messages like, "see my profile" and think that people will contact you just doesn't work. Write and attempt to bring out the writer/poet in you. Paint words into pictures that will capture the imagination of men and that will attract them want to meet you.

A great mistake is to send out "form letters" -- like direct mailers. This is an insult to any educated person's intelligence.

Personalize the mails—make it specific to the person you are writing to. Remember this is an attempt to find Mr. Right not an exercise in answering circulars. Ideally, letters should be conversations where one discovers each other through words.

Making maximal use of the membership by contacting men at random—the idea is to use the money paid to the fullest. Think what is that you really want---correspond with many men or find the one you want to cultivate /build a relationship with.

Take the time to read all the profiles that fit your list of "The Ideal Man," then narrow down a list of a select few—write to these, wait until they answer, try and find out as much as you can about them and then if you still have not found anyone start the process all over again.

Don't write a haphazard profile and using a randomly selected photo. It is a mistake not to submit a photo with your profile. There are men out there who never contact a woman they cannot see. When you don't include a photo, most people assume you have something to hide. According to sites people who post photos get ten times more contacts than those that don't. Use a recent photo and one that flatters you. If you can, have a professional take the photo. Don't post sleazy photo of yourself unless you're looking for a sleazy relationship! Choose a nice, natural photo of yourself don't use one that includes other people. The main photo should be a "head and shoulders" one - a close up. If the site allows more than one photo, then you can be more adventurous include, full length shots, pets, kids, and so on.

Tips on Choosing Your Online Photo:

* ❖ If you don't have any suitable recent photos, arrange to go out with friends. Relax and have fun. Get your friends to take lots of photos of you. Hopefully, you'll get at least one that you're happy to post.

* ❖ If you have a photo of yourself in a social environment, use that one. It will give a better impression than one of you seated on your sofa at home.

* ❖ Don't post photos of yourself looking unhappy, drunk, hung-over, lonely, or on a bad hair day!

* ❖ Avoid expensive accessories for your photo. It sends a high maintenance signal.

* ❖ If you want to post multiple photos, make sure that they're varied and interesting.

* ❖ Avoid multiple photos taken at the same time. Don't use it as an opportunity to demonstrate in six different ways how attractive you are. It should be an opportunity to convey the fact that you've got an interesting life.

❖ It's OK to change your photo from time to time if you come up with better ones, or if they get more than a year old.

❖ Even if a photo is a professional one make it look casual. Never wear high fashion garments or accessories.

Dating sites often give guidelines for posting photos. For example, Yahoo personal says, Do not post pictures if:

❖ You are not central in the photo.

❖ The picture is off focus/hazy.

❖ Does not convey an image of the "true you."

❖ Have too many people.

❖ The picture is old not current.

One must post photos that: have a smile, show your eyes clearly, and represent in no uncertain terms you as you are. The photograph must allow your personality to shine through.

Never use photos where you are dressed in skimpy clothes or are heavily made up—ones that make you look like a bimbo (unless that is what you are). Coming through as sexy with oomph is not going to get you what you desire.

A frequent online dating blunder is negativity---feeling that the whole exercise of online dating is a futile effort. Believe me, nine out of ten things don't work the first few weeks or months—it may even take a year.

Never be discouraged and give up—hope, patience, and persistence are what will get you to your goal. Pause a few days and take a look at "what needs correction" ---read through successful profiles and compare them to yours. Make changes in your profile as well as criteria of the "man" perhaps your list of musts is too stringent. Be flexible and you will meet many who may come up to your expectations.

Be open minded and friendly. There is a special person waiting for you –you just need to tread the right path.

CHAPTER 4: CREATING AN EYE-CATCHING HEADLINE

The headline draws the attention of online dating browsers...It is important for you to learn how to create a headline that will not only be eye-catching, but interest potential prospects.

Personal headlines on most sites can be of 100 characters. A poor headline can negate a good username. It is the headline that gives a first impression. A personal headline should not indicate that you are a bore, selfish, a fool, or scatterbrain. If the headline is repulsive or boring, rest assured, you will not get many queries.

A personal headline often determines the kind of person you want to meet. If you are seeking a serious relationship then your headline must not indicate "seeking fun and frolic."

Avoid done to death phrases as well as cute ones. Adventurous, unique, and wonderful are all cliché.

The secret is to incorporate a little about yourself or to be creative and clever. Commonly coined ones are:

❖ "I am a Lady."

❖ "Ask me if you can."

❖ "Life can be a path of roses."

- ❖ "Poet."

- ❖ "Sailing Smooth."

- ❖ "Polite, serious, and creative."

The headline is the most important tool of an online profile—pay attention to coining it.

- ❖ Let it lead men into your profile. It should tease and intrigue.

- ❖ Avoid negativity ---refrain from using words like "no."

- ❖ Incorporate word play—be creative and quick.

- ❖ Snappy headlines attract attention.

A headline should grab attention—it should be succinct and dead on—summing up what you are about. It should invite – tweak their curiosity to read your profile. Use word play—internal rhyme or a pun.

Examples:

"Let's race the wind!"

"Looking for sparring partner!"

"Package deal—me, kids, pets!"

"Geek by day, poet by night!"

"Explore the world with me!"

"Walk to the beat of a new drummer!"

"Want to play doubles!"

"First date in a dozen years!"

"Think Advertising..."

Remember how the catchy phrases create imagery. The concept is similar here you are the product to be marketed. Just as "rich and creamy" conjures up images of swirls of ice cream, so also the headline should bring forth an image of an attractive, friendly woman.

As far as dating sites are concerned the most prominent things after the "photo" is the headline. Studies indicate men have a tendency to make snap judgments, so the headline should project a positive image of you.

Negativity must be avoided, never include words like lonely, companion, seeking comfort, rich and handsome. Avoidable are impressions of your being glamorous, seeking a life of leisure, or being high maintenance.

Keys are: Originality, uniqueness, be concise, positivity, fresh and candid...

Originality, candidness, humor, and freshness are welcome. The secret is in being attractive as well as mysterious. Men love challenges.

CHAPTER 5: PRODUCING AN APPEALING PROFILE

Creating an appealing online profile is the key foundation of successful online dating. Your profile informs any dating prospects of your characteristics, what you're looking for and what kinds of individual you are. Basic information includes: Appearance, interests, age, profession, hobbies, likes, dislikes, etc...This helps your online prospects make out your compatibility with each other. But remember, what really matters is your personal profile – it's what sets you apart from a zillion others. You must take advantage of this and highlight the key elements of yourself.

List all of your passions, likes and dislikes in an interesting way. Give your readers an idea what you're seeking, without making it sound too straight-forward. And before posting your profile, make sure to review your profile and get a friend or relative to read through it and get their honest opinion.

Most sites will ask for details of age, height, ethnicity, religion, eye color, hair color, occupation, education, smoking preference, favorite hobbies, a description of your personality, what you are looking for in a man, whether you are seeking a casual relationship, a friendship, a short-term fling, long term romance, or marriage, what is important to you in a man, your value system, beliefs, specific affiliations and more.

To be successful in love, the profile must present you in the best light and give would be suitors a glimpse or inkling of what makes you tick and how to win you over. Write as though you are in a conversation with someone. Imagine sitting across a table and telling a dashing, handsome man all about yourself.

A profile is generally of 200-250 words. Write around 150- 200 words about yourself and around 50-100 words can be devoted to describing the kind of person you are looking for.

Remember to Include:

Personal details - Where you live, whether you are open to changing your place of residence, where you have traveled and so on.

Discuss your profession – Career history as well as future plans.

Speak about past experiences and relationships. Talk about children if you have them. Be sure to mention whether you are hoping to have children or do not want any.

Tell the truth - In case you have any serious health problem be sure to write about it. People rarely like surprises.

Your personal background - One should also mention any religious or political affiliations that you may have.

The type of relationship you'd like - Mention what kind of relationship you are looking for—long term or short term.

When writing a profile one must:

❖ Be honest and truthful. Never fabricate scenarios or stories – ultimately if you want a serious relationship the man must know and get to like the real you.

❖ Don't hide facts like your age or whether you have children.

❖ It is best to show or prove not just state facts. Instead of saying "I am funny" show you are funny by weaving in a real-life incident or joke about an experience that is etched in your memory. This will give a glimpse of you and make your profile distinct from others.

❖ Write for the "audience" not for yourself. Never give too much or too little information.

❖ Never be superficial.

❖ Adjectives mean nothing, avoid them if you can ---words like nice, smart, kind, warm, loving, ambitious, go getter, family oriented are meaningless words.

❖ While speaking of interests try and include details. For example if you like hiking—then mention where all you have been and where you plan to or look forward to going.

This gives more information than listing a long line of interests—biking, tennis, dogs, movies, and so on.

❖ Don't use clichés in your profile; every other person is "cute/ cuddly/ tall/ looking for a friend/understanding companion," make your profile simple, clear, and concise. Bragging is another "NO"—please do avoid subjective evaluations.

❖ Try and define yourself positively—let the profile show who/what you are. There is no point in repeatedly stating what you want or your future aspirations.

When in doubt, seek the help of professionals. Many dating sites offer professional profile writing /reviewing help.

The profile is what creates a first impression, so write one that aims to be different and is appealing as well as honest. Remember this is what a man will read before deciding should I contact her or not.

The profile should give an insight to who you really are. A great profile will increase greatly your chances of linking up with the Mr. Right—a man who meets all your needs and is not just compatible in an analytical way but is a man who is genuine and wants to know more about you—get to know the real you.

We all know it is not a perfect world and even in online dating one can encounter undesirables. To protect yourself from unwanted problems:

- ❖ **Do Not** list your address.

- ❖ **Do Not** mention your phone number.

- ❖ **Do Not** give away where you love to go—a bar or coffee house or library that you frequent.

- ❖ **Do Not** enumerate any vital statistics.

- ❖ **Do Not** mention financial details.

- ❖ **Do Not** indicate where you work or shop.

- ❖ **Do Not** ever say where you work out.

Until you are sure you are ready to know a man better and are sure about his credentials never reveal personal information.

CHAPTER 6: A REAL STORY

Online dating is all about knowing how to present the "Real You" to the world. To do that, you must know yourself well...There should be no layers or hidden components. Wouldn't you be upset if you read an online profile and met the individual who turned out to be very different from what their profile says? It happens all the time.

So, if you are serious about dating and being successful you must desist from penning a fairy tale or living it. Fabricating incidents or stories is just not done. If you are really seeking to get close to a man then you will not be able to carry on living a lie however small forever.

Be honest with yourself—just as you are suspicious /wary of people so also men who are trying online dating. Contradictions are unnecessary and very negative. You will agree that "we are what we are" and cannot by using mere words turn into glamorous women or someone adventurous.

White lies and contradictions are guarantees of being dumped. Once a man realizes he cannot trust you he will steer clear. Not only that your reputation will spread like wildfire.

One thing that is crucial is that "we have to live with ourselves and be happy." So, it is best to be with a man who accepts you for what you are and does not expect you to change. Never be afraid to say "I detest plays/or fancy clothes are not ME/ or I love balloon rides."

Relationships only work when a man and woman live the life of two distinct individuals and yet share bonds, love, and common interests. There must be personal space and freedom in a relationship. Otherwise bitterness will creep in.

So, be yourself and seek a man who suits you best. He may not be drop dead handsome but may have a sense of humor, care about the little things in life, and appreciate you.

Sit down and ask yourself, "What am I seeking." And, write down all that flows from your mind. Put the book away and after a day or two repeat the exercise -points that are common to both days are probably what are most important. Others will be the result of moods.

Take the time and make the effort of looking through profiles as well as experiences posted by other women. You will gain a fairly good idea of what works and what does not. I'm not suggesting that you copy someone else's profile word for word, but you can get ideas of good phrases and the type of stuff they include.

Next, read through profiles posted by men and make a list of what appeals to you. Gain an understanding of what they're looking for (apart from the obvious physical characteristics), and you will be able to include some aspects in your profile—

be sure they pertain to who you are and not to an idea of you in your imagination. Don't go over the top, though --if you say that you love sitting in front of the TV, watching all types of sport, whilst eating a ready meal with a few cans of beer, you'll probably find a suitable man, but may not have a blissful life!

Avoid negativity or sounding doubtful---don't start with "I'm surprised I'm doing this ....", or "I've never done this before ...." You're opening line is important, so don't waste it on an excuse or an apology.

Be specific about your lifestyle and interests. Rather than listing hobbies give specific examples – I have trekked the Andes, or sailed through the keys, or put together a classic car in our garage with my brother. Specifics paint word pictures of the "true you."

Don't come across as a dreary, lonely woman. If your life is like that make an effort to change it by adopting some hobbies, going out with friends, traveling, and doing interesting things. Make a concerted effort to be a "new you." Discover yourself—life is too short to be spent going to work and sitting at home.

Be positive, energetic, open minded, and a giver. Never be a doormat and allow people to push you around.

Make realistic goals. However don't come across as pushy or seeking permanency like marriage. Allow a friendship/relationship to develop before thinking about marriage. Men are spooked at the thought of commitment and will turn tail and run like a trapped animal.

Do speak of past relationships but don't let that be the most important aspect of your existence. Never compare the present to the past. Leave what is past behind, learn from it and move forward. Don't make the mistake of comparing men—my ex husband loved steak, or my previous boyfriend was a great dancer is "ugly and sad."

Let your story be a "happy one" be a woman who has savored life and is ready to share the joys.

Quick Chapter Review:

❖ Ask yourself what you're seeking. Remember you are in control!

❖ Don't skim, but carefully take the time to read other users profiles to see which one is most compatible with yours.

❖ Avoid negativity while writing your profile

❖ Be specific. The more details you have, the more appealing you come across.

- ❖ Don't look desperate.

- ❖ Be Positive and Energetic.

- ❖ Be realistic and make real goals.

- ❖ Don't be afraid to speak of past relationships

Chapter 7: Finding that Perfect Someone

Every woman wants to find the man of her dreams. The fact is you have to be practical when choosing your mate. If you're looking for an absolute stud, with a big bank account and a 4-garage door mansion – you have to be sensible.

Learn about the art of giving and caring. Romance is not the superficial aspects of dating - flowers, gifts, romantic evenings, and wooing. It is about showing you care, small endearing gestures, deep understanding of even a glance, and a synchronization of minds as well as soul.

To be practical one must set goals/parameters.

Jot down:

"What kind of man do I want?"

"How do I perceive my future—do children play a role?"

"What does a relationship mean to me personally? Is it caring, friendship, passion, being physical or mental compatibility?"

What do you seek in a man? Is it, humor, loyalty, fairness, respect, warmth, intelligence, kindness, integrity, honesty, tenderness, pride, chivalry?

- ❖ What should the ideal man look like?

- ❖ Should he smoke and drink.

- ❖ What are 5 things I abhor in men?

- ❖ What are 5 things I find pleasing and attractive?

- ❖ Do I want a single man or will I accept one who has been in past relationships—divorced/widowed?

- ❖ What kind of profession should he be in?

Create a profile as a ready reference. Use this to compare profiles you read online with. Narrow down the choices. Be sure you know how to distinguish between Mr. Right and Mr. Wrong.

According to experts in dating:

- ❖ A man who drinks heavily, is loud and manner less is definitely Mr. Wrong.

- ❖ A good man would be well mannered and considerate and limit his drinking. He would not brag about bar hopping, drinking buddies, or bouts. He would never drink and drive a date home.

- ❖ A less than perfect man is one who is selfish, self obsessed, spends all his time talking about himself, his work, personal experiences, how he is a stud -- a total braggart.

❖ A man who is serious about dating and wishes to further the meet will try and find out as much as he can about you. He will share important aspects of his life with you, and try and give insights into his likes/dislikes, hopes as well as aspirations.

❖ The wrong kind will flirt with other women while he sits with you, let his attention wander, speak about how he finds 'x' lovely or 'y' a turn on. He will brag about his conquests every chance he gets. Self-obsessed he will never think beyond himself.

❖ An ideal man will not flirt unless he knows you well, he will never pass lewd remarks, or make passes, or advertise his conquests.

❖ The wrong kind is flashy and will flaunt their money as well as wealth/position. If he is handsome and has a good physique he will be obsessed by it —constantly glance in mirrors, comb his locks, and wink at passersby and so on.

❖ A man who is just perfect will be interested in more than a physical relationship—he will try and understand what makes you tick and find out whether the two of you have any common grounds.

Watch out for men who:

❖ Lie to you.

❖ Pressure you to meet them immediately.

❖ Are persistent about finding out personal information but do not reveal anything about themselves.

❖ Do not give accurate information about their age, marital status, having children, profession and so on.

❖ Who do not want to speak on the phone.

❖ Become a nuisance and pester you to speed things up.

Try and strike a balance. However, do allow for a little flexibility. A man may not match all your requirements but even if he matches say 60% then you must try and get to know him better.

Broaden your base—this will offer you greater choice. But do not compromise on things like "no smoking"-- a man who has smoked and been independent for years together is not likely to give up his habits because you say so.

It is not tall, dark, and handsome you must look for its kindness, caring, and intelligence. Very often, if physical attributes receive more attention then what you are likely to get is a man looking for a fling and not willing to offer any commitments.

If you are clear in your mind "what you want" then everything else becomes relatively easy. Please have a realistic opinion of yourself—if you are approaching thirty and fighting the flab, have a sprinkling of grey hair you are not going to land a man who is dashing, drives a Ferrari, and looks like a Hollywood dream. Try and match what you are to the man ---seek compatibility.

CHAPTER 8: STAYING ACTIVE FOR POSITIVE RESULTS

Most people make the common mistake of just filling in their profile and forgeting about it, waiting for people to contact them. Sure, they may get some inquires and occasional questions, but they may not be aware of what you are looking for.

Be proactive and take your life into your own hands—after all who knows what you want better than you yourself.

Understand what dating fundamentals are:

❖ **The attitude must be right**—change for the better and be positive.

❖ **Spending all the waking hours at work or at home will not help you meet Mr. Right.** You will just be craving for companionship.

❖ **Effort goes into finding Mr. Right**—unless your Mr. Right is the mail man or pizza delivery boy.

❖ **What one needs is motivation** --- overcome the lethargy and get going.

❖ **Forget the past and seek the future**—aim to be positive I know rejection and break ups hurt and are emotionally wringing.

- ❖ **All of us have scars** that smart stemming from broken relationships and unfulfilled dreams --- no one is spared—so stop moping and begin the search.

- ❖ **Look good and stand tall**—and you will find that the world of men perceives you differently.

- ❖ **Get rid of the words "no" and "can't" from your vocabulary**—adopt nothing is impossible and I can do this.

- ❖ **Fight negativity** and single blessedness.

- ❖ **Reach out for the sky**---fulfill your dreams. Prioritize your life—personal goals are as important as professional ones.

- ❖ **The entire world is full of opportunities**-- just grab them.

Shrug that huge chip off your shoulder --- a large and important part of dating success is ATTITUDE.

Successful Ways to Tackle Dating

Make an action plan. For example you can decide, must make at least 3-4 new friends by the end of 30 days. Always seek out people you are comfortable with—do not aim for men who seem to have stepped right out of a film---tall, dark, and handsome.

Adopt relaxation methods - deep breathing, tai chi, or music, or gardening. If you remain calm and collected, you will be able to see the world more clearly.

Activity groups are great for meeting like-minded people. Pursue an activity you like—biking, hiking, photography, poetry reading, pottery classes, cooking classes, or even therapy groups. Once you are a regular, the ice will break and you will find yourself making many new friends.

Find topics one can easily talk about - the weather, traffic, bakeries, food, and music - all general interest ones. If you choose a specialty subject like say sculpture you may be excluding several people from participating.

Only plan a date when you have identified a "likely" Mr. X and formed a friendship with him. Make all efforts to find out as much as you can about him.

Plan a date down to the last detail - what you will wear, when you will return, what you will say, how you will position yourself as well as your hands. Be sure not to fidget it conveys discomfort.

Take care - always inform a close friend or family member where you are going and with whom. Leave a contact number where you can be reached. Precautions have saved many lives.

Once you have decided that cyber dating is your path, sit down every day, or twice a week, or in the weekends and read profiles of men who have a membership on the site. Make a list of "probable men."

Then after a few days, read through the short listed profiles once again to make sure that your choice in the first instance was right.

If yes, then you must:

❖ Use tools like hot lists, smiles, virtual flowers, friendships, on the site to express an interest. One can choose to send a smile to a profile to say subtly I am interested in knowing you better. You can offer to send an e-mail if the person is interested and offer to accept "collect call e-mails."

❖ Make contact by using information in the profile to break the ice, "I read that you have sailed the Florida Keys—I too went there three years ago and got caught in a squall!" Make the contact interesting it does not have to be—"hi, I am xxx, I like yyy."

❖ Weave a little humor into the message – laughter makes many friends.

❖ Show you are interested overcome shyness and fears to say, "I liked your profile—so please do read mine!"

❖ Make messaging like a conversation – weave in questions as well as answers it must be a dialogue not a monologue.

❖ Read up on the art of cyber flirting and conversation starters for the tired and weary. Be creative.

❖ Progress by e-mailing one another and chatting online— try and find out as much as you can about the man, his lifestyle, experiences, hopes, and despairs. Try and keep your eyes and ears open to discrepancies—white lies, changed story lines, and so on.

❖ If you are fairly certain you like the man, suggest a phone conversation – it   is an opportunity to find out how he speaks. And, if you are astute, conversations and voice inflections can reveal a lot.

❖ Once you are sure –then consider meeting the man in a public place if possible in a group. Read up on safety concerns in dating. Go ahead met the man casually and then progress from there.

Keep in mind that every contact may not become fruitful. So you need to use your membership to the fullest and read profiles as well as contact possible men over a period of time until Mr. Right comes along.

It would be wise not to make decisions based on first impressions. Many a time, a person may turn out to be interesting once you get to know them. Men like women can be shy and inhibited—things change once they are comfortable with you.

Tips:

❖ Women can take the initiative and contact a man.

❖ Make use of the "search criteria" options offered by sites. If in doubt, use the help options. View the FAQ section; most commonly asked questions are answered here.

❖ Statistics reveal that successful online daters view more than a hundred profiles each month. Don't be disappointed if you do not meet with immediate success. The key is to strive and always keep hope alive in your heart.

❖ Don't just go by how they look, gain an insight into their character by reading their profiles and by asking relevant questions.

❖ And once you are comfortable with a man you can even initiate the first phone call /meeting. Some men just need a nudge.

❖ The 20:1 rule according to users is applicable to online dating---for every 20 profiles you contact you can expect to receive one response.

❖ One can increase the chances by posting:

- ➤ An eye-catching picture.

- ➤ Writing a one in million profile.

- ➤ By asking questions and revealing what you find interesting in a profile.

If you adopt these strategies you can hope to double or quadruple your online dating responses.

While contacting people you will be wise to avoid: jocks, mamma's boys, and field players—otherwise you are headed for heartbreak.

Using chat is integral to online dating. It is a service one can use to get to know people. Use the facility but exercise caution.

- ❖ Before you join a chat pause a moment to observe –get a feel of the chat room, size up the chatters, follow the pattern of their conversations. And, only if you are comfortable join them.

- ❖ Introduce yourself and say "hi" in a friendly way.

- ❖ Avoid gossip and criticism.

- ❖ Ignore people who are rude, lewd, and disruptive.

- ❖ Use emoticons, SMS lingo, and audibles while chatting. Familiarize yourself with them.

❖ You can select a certain day, time, as well as chat room in which to meet your friends.

❖ If you become a part of a group or forum do welcome new people. Expand your group that way you will meet many more people.

❖ Host a chat event.

❖ Choose topics that are current, interesting, and attractive to all.

Online sites will have as members, all kinds of people---some are there just for fun, others are wackos, yet others are serious about meeting their true love, some join to pass the time and have no intention of taking the relationship forward beyond e-mail friendship.

It takes all kind to make the world but most people come to online sites to find a date and make a connection with like-minded people.

Make an effort to look for people with similar needs to yours. Don't answer profiles that are looking for a casual relationship or describe a "Baywatch" babe as their ideal woman.

Make at least 2-3 phone calls before progressing to a meet the person date.

The keys to being a "hit" are:

❖ Write e-mails that are friendly and positive.
❖ Don't mention the past.
❖ Never come across as arrogant or a snob.
❖ Never mislead your dating prospects.
❖ Be candid, friendly, and honest.
❖ Project yourself in a "good light."

Chapter 9: Should He Stay or Should He Go

How does one decide whether a man is worth a try? It is a hard decision to make and really depends on what you are seeking from life and a man.

The basis of life in general and dating in particular is the answer to a question you must ask yourself "what do I expect from a man?"

This will put things in perspective and answer is 'X' Mr. Right?

For most women the "ideal" man is one who:

* Has a sense of humor.
* Is not critical of others.
* Does not see himself as god's gift to women.
* Has a deep sense of fairness and loyalty.
* Respects women and does not see them as "bare foot and pregnant."
* Is kindness and warmth personified.
* Is intelligent and appreciates an intelligent and successful woman.

In order to determine whether Mr. X is the guy you are looking for, you need to be open-minded and view him as an individual separate from your dad, ex-husband, or previous lover/boyfriend. You must be willing to communicate – unless lines of communication are kept open you will never be able to discover each other.

Have the right mindset—is looks and money important or are they by the by? Men are astute and know immediately when someone is chasing them not for themselves but for their wealth. Decide —it is the man who is important not drop dead good looks or being rich. Look for quality not materialistic things. Try and match the man to what you yourself are. It is love and commitment you need to aim for.

Put the man before other future plans like having kids—many men will run if they think all you want to do is have kids before your biological clock stops ticking. Men like to feel needed for themselves. So never discuss setting up a home with a yard, a nursery, or which school/college your kids will go to.

Be attractive at all times—it boosts your confidence. Have a makeover, do your hair, wear attractive clothes. You never know when or how you may meet the man—suppose you are chatting online and the conversation veers towards turning on the "webcam" —imagine being in a duster coat or unattractive t-shirt.

According to relationship advisers', being dressed well boosts confidence levels and makes one feel pretty on the inside and outside.

Leave the past way behind —when chatting only speak of what you are, what makes you tick, what you enjoy and so on. Also try and find out as much as you can about the man—see if his "perfect woman" list matches what you are.

Glance beyond good looks and determine how good he is at relationships by finding out how he relates with his mother, sisters, cousins, and people at the office. You can tell if he is caring and considerate by drawing out answers to questions placed cleverly while chatting.

A man is worth a try if:

❖ He matches most of your must have list.

❖ You look forward to his e-mails and chatting online.

❖ His photo is attractive.

❖ You have a few common interests.

❖ He is admiring of your achievements and activities.

❖ He has complimented you in his e-mails and shown interest.

❖ He is considerate and lets you know when he is away or busy so that you are not left wondering why he has not replied to the mail.

❖ Is willing to speak with you on the phone.

❖ Does not seem to be hiding anything and is open with his answers.

Once you know for sure you are interested, do arrange to speak over the phone. You need not reveal your personal number but use facilities provided by dating sites.

If you are nervous about what to say read up articles on dating and speaking over the phone---treat the man like a friend and not a potential lover. This will alleviate uneasiness to a large extent.

Gather courage and forge ahead—be prepared and accept disappointments, it is not the end of the world, around every corner is a rainbow.

CHAPTER 10: FIRST CONTACT

Dating has become very complex, personally and business wise. Online sites compete with each other to provide users with comprehensive facilities. Activities and Services are also organized to test users and their compatibility.

Once the profile is posted and fee paid the adventure of online dating begins...

The first step is to try the quick searches and to read matches sent by the site itself. Next make use of special services offered by the site like:

❖ Smart selection where you find a profile that interests you, then click on smart selection or show similar profiles button---the site will send you other profiles that are similar to the one you like. All you have to do is sit back and relax. Such facilities under different names are offered by most 'top' dating sites.

❖ One can do a "key word" search—use words that are of importance to you—fishing, writing, plays, acting, and so on. Use common interests to locate possible men.

❖ Search using specifics--fill in specific criteria like: age, height, location, body type, hair/eye color and so on. Then save these specifics and search using them as base line.

❖ Use "break the ice" option—when you spy a profile you like, click on "break the ice." Pen a message that is in synchrony with your mood. The site will forward the message along with your profile for consideration.

Apart from being databases of men and women seeking partners, sites take dating a step further by putting 'filters' in place to weed out unsuitable candidates. So, you can be reasonable sure about the profiles you are vetting.

Online sites allow you a chance to know a lot about possible suitors—you can ask questions about hobbies, career, education, family, relationships, political affiliation, religious beliefs, and more.

Many of them have a system by which they match profiles, and then mail suitable ones for your consideration. They also lend anonymity - you need not reveal personal details until you really want to or have to.

You can ignore or delete e-mails that you are just not interested in. You do not have to undergo the agony of saying "sorry no." And since you "meet" possible suitors from behind a computer you are able to overcome fears as well as shyness.

Unlike dates where you meet one to one, a dating site allows you to look through hundreds of profiles without any pressures. There are innovations on a few sites—you can send emoticons, virtual flowers, and more to possible daters showing that you are interested. You can send winks, smiles, as well as virtual flowers to show interest. You can make the initiate and contact a profile that interests you--- say I read your profile and found x, y, and z, interesting. Be sure to mention something about yourself and weave in factors about him that you found interesting. Weave in casual comments as well as humor. Never sound needy or desperate.

They offer online chats as well as forums where you can actually virtually meet men. At first you must just observe how these work, choose one with a subject that is of interest to you. Communicate naturally and honestly. Use a name that describes you but not your true identity. Converse casually and as though you are in conversation with someone. Be polite and respectful, if you are wrong about something be magnanimous and accept it. There is no harm in admitting that you don't know something. Try not to bring up past relationships or experiences. Have fun and look forward to making new friends.

Having facilities from where you can both send e-mails and receive them without revealing personal details. This is a safety feature to protect you from unwanted suitors. Finally, they have systems where "daters" can speak to one another without revealing their locations or phone numbers. The site protects you at all times.

However, even while using an online dating site you must ensure your own safety. Never reveal personal details, workplace addresses, phone numbers, or bank account details, it is best if you don't speak about where you shop, have lunch, or spend evenings.

You should only speak about these once you are confident about a man and have had the time to "check him out."

Online dating sites can be rewarding, fun, exciting and a secure environment for meeting new people. But the most reliable safety measure that anyone can take or have is common sense; trust your basic instincts more than anything else.

Always Remember To:

❖ Choose a creative user name. This will ensure that men searching through profiles will pause, be intrigued, and want to know more. You must be different stand out from the hundreds of profiles.

❖ Coin a flirty headline. It should pack a punch and yet be sweet and short. You will never capture a man's attention if you just select one from the many samples posted online. Try not being aggressive or bossy or simpering — witty works.

- ❖ Men are visual creatures and are mostly attracted by appearance. Be sure to post a photo that flatters you.

- ❖ Respond to e-mails with care. Avoid writing a novel—men have short attention spans. So, answer questions, be witty, ask a few questions—make it short and sweet not a saga.

- ❖ Write responses to everyone. That way you will meet many more possible suitors. Your response percentage should be at least 80%.

Navigate successfully by:

- ❖ Staying happy, confident, and positive while e-mailing or IM ing men. Don't overwhelm the other person by coming on too strong—keep it light and friendly. Be sure to pace yourself.

- ❖ Use the photos posted to make an opinion of a man— there is a saying that a picture can speak a thousand words. Read up on how to look at pictures and read character.

- ❖ Never rush things along—control the pace of the online relationship, never hurry and make plans to meet before you know 'enough' about a person.

- ❖ Before meeting take another step of caution, speak on the phone at least 2-3 times. Women can make suggestions too! Don't speak from a personal phone or mobile use the safe services provided by dating services.

❖ Listen to your heart—if you get negative thoughts or bad vibes then end the contact.

❖ When you are ready to meet in person do so in a public place—make it a four some it is safer.

Take what online dating has to offer with a smile---there are so many avenues and possibilities. You can if you do things right meet Mr. Right---a man with whom you feel a connection, there is chemistry, and you have lots in common.

A great fulfilling romance is one for life's purest joys. When you meet a partner with whom you can share values, attitudes, love, as well as grief you would have found your dream.

To achieve this you must have a sense of purpose. Be ready to have fun and head in the "right" direction. Take dating slowly—those who date for two years before marrying have successful marriages as they have worked all the kinks out and are sure where they are headed. The saying "haste makes waste" applies to dating.

Have a realistic expectation. There are no such things like Prince Charming or Sir Galahad –men are men and have good traits as well as bad ones. Try and strike a balance. Find a man who cares and is understanding but don't expect him to give up "buddy nights" or fishing because you are now a part of his life.

The "key" is look forward to: sharing a few interests and to having separate ones.

Be responsible and address any serious issues right in the beginning. Problems like alcoholism, drug dependency, temper tantrums, smoking, emotional dysfunctions, or physical abuse never resolve later.

Date with your eye open—be aware of the plus as well as minus points. Don't rush into passionate relationships. Listen to your mind and heart.

Follow online etiquette and have a great time.

CHAPTER 11: THE FIRST PHONE CALL

A phone call, according to experts can reveal a lot about a person. It gives insights into a person's character as well as social skills.

Several online sites have what is known as "Private call" phone services –this allows men and women to speak to each other without exchanging their personal numbers. If a person is not reachable, the system repeatedly dials until both parties are connected. The "anonymous" phone call services give "daters" a chance to see if there is chemistry without risking safety.

Such serves are simple to use:

❖ A dater can set their availability then click select on profiles they want to talk to.

❖ The other person has the right to OK the call or refuse it.

❖ If the man accepts the call then the system handles the calling with proactive.

❖ The party who invites is billed for the call.

Chat on the phone as many times as you feel the need. Listen attentively, what do you hear in the background—pets, children, silence, traffic noises? Often noises can verify what a person has told you.

It is safe not to use your personal phone until you are sure the man is dependable.

Remember to block caller ID –this prevents disclosure of the number you are calling from.

If the number you are calling is an 800 # number then your phone number will appear on the man's phone bill.

Take the trouble to call directory assistance and ensure that your date's number matches the information he gave. Directory assistance will also tell you if X has an unlisted number.

Call when least expected –gauge the reaction, it is delight/surprise, or does he show irritation, does another female answer the phone. Without becoming a nuisance try and find out if Mr. X has something to hide.

Listen attentively—notice any inconsistencies or odd behaviors. Look out for evasive or changing answers to the same question. Listen with your heart trust yourself—if you find anything uncomfortable or something is niggling walk away before you are hurt.

Master the art of asking questions—find out where he was born and grew up, where he works, does he participate in community activities. Does he have siblings /pets? What are his leisure activities? Don't shoot questions at him but weave them into seemingly harmless conversation.

If you are shy and become tongue tied when actually speaking to a person, here is what you should do —well before you answer the phone or dial his number jot down for your ready reference a few points to guide you along the way.

Easy conversation topics are the weather, work experiences, movies, celebrity news, and so on. Avoid topics that can create a controversy.

Never ring up a possible date when he is at work and leave a vague message on the phone—gather up courage and speak to the man , after all he is among those you have chosen to start a possible relationship with.

Before calling, read through the man's profile as well as the mails you have exchanged—they will give you insights on what to speak about. Then, make notes of interesting points that can be woven into the conversation. Think what has happened in the last week that is "news?"

Use discoveries, mysteries, new movies, and plays as well as best sellers as conversation pieces and highlight using a fluorescent marker which ones you plan to use.

Similarly write down a few points about yourself—just like cue cards at a play—to help you make the conversation flow smoothly. One can speak about funny things that happened at work. Great conversation can be woven around: blooms in your garden, happenings at work, a trip you took or want to take, sports, book releases, exhibitions and so on.

If gourmet cooking is a common interest then there is nothing like "food and wine" to find common tastes and oodles to talk about.

You could paint word pictures of a typical day; speak about the kids if you have them. Share your aspirations/dreams. Be candid.

Before ending the call decide, would I like to speak to this man again if yes then suggest, "Hi I have to go now but we could talk again on Friday—how about that!"

Telephone etiquette demands:

❖ The ideal time to call is early evening –not before 6.00 pm and not after 9.00pm.

❖ Never call from a car, while stuck in traffic, or from a crowded bar or office.

❖ Find a quite peaceful place to make your call from. Be sure you are relaxed and in the right mood.

❖ The call should not be too long or short—if it is too long one can run out of things to say and too short is rude.

❖ Strike a balance, make general conversation and discover each other. If you enjoy the chat then make arrangements to talk again.

❖ Use the right kind of voice—clear your throat before speaking, don't speak too fast or slow, put emotion into the tones.

❖ Let not the voice come through as business-like or clipped.

❖ Speak slowly; try not to be nervous, as this will become evident in your voice. Voices convey as much as body language does--- convey happiness and enthusiasm not fear and doubts.

CHAPTER 12: HOW TO HANDLE REJECTION

Romance is not always successful. Fairy tales and love stories are always buttering things up and are full of exaggerated, unrequited love. One thing's for sure, there are people who will befriend us, and others who will not.

The fact is, not everyone will find Mr. Perfect. Heck, there's no such thing as a perfect man. Just as we do not accept every man who comes along as Mr. Right, so also in the case of men, what we are may not be what they are seeking. Rejection is only a natural part of the dating scene. This being so "rejection" must be accepted as integral to dating and in the right spirit.

Easy steps that will help us cure rejection are:

❖ **First admit that you are scared.** And that you need to deal with the situation.

❖ **Quantify the fear/shyness/self-doubt.** Try and find out on a scale of 1-10 where your apprehensions stand.

❖ **Confront the worst thing that could happen.** Be it rejection, humiliation, or being made a fool of. Emotional or physical hurt is a part of loving.

- ❖ **Cope with it in an organized and methodical way**—say I am not going to let my mind/feelings pull me down. I am out to conquer.

- ❖ **Join a support group.** Go for counseling and deal with the situation.

- ❖ **Don't be ashamed or inhibited to discuss your true feelings** with family/friends /others in a similar situation.

- ❖ **Use all available resources** to conquer fear/self doubt.

- ❖ **Set ego aside** and stop believing "I am god's gift to men."

Handling heartbreak is not easy you need to gather yourself together and move on. Here are a few ways you can cope:

- ❖ **Get it out of your system.** Don't let emotions be bottled up inside and turn into resentment and bitterness.

- ❖ **Cry, scream, vent your frustration at a dummy or hedge, and feel sorry for yourself as much as you want.** Do so until there is no sadness left and you have worked the feeling of "rejection" out of your system.

- ❖ **Focus on everyday activities.** Take one step at a time. Let the future take care of itself.

- ❖ **Give yourself space and time to heal.** The biggest mistake would be to plunge in at once into another relationship.

- ❖ **Take a deep breath** and say I am going to look forward.

- ❖ **Be positive, think happy thoughts,** fill you day with activities and people so that you have no time to brood.

- ❖ **Don't abandon hope** –perhaps the man who rejected you was not the ideal man for you.

- ❖ **Early rejection is better** than heartbreak.

- ❖ **Let not rejection become a fear** be strong convince yourself, "I am a wonderful person."

- ❖ **Join new interests or activities.** Many hobbies are such that they are popular, which means you stand a good chance of making many friends.

Rejection hurts and makes one sad but misery will not get you anywhere—you must move on. I know it is hard as most women are vulnerable and suffer from the 'pain' of rejection.

One way to handle the situation is to stop thinking less of yourself —being critical and seeking approval. This makes us open to rejection and hurt.

Accept this is what I am and I am proud of who I am.

Never blame yourself for being rejected. In fact try and think "too bad for him" he lost a wonderful caring woman.

Work out a rejection contingency plan--- believe me rejection can be a blessing in disguise.

❖ Anyone who does not appreciate you as a person is not worth it.

❖ A man who truly cares will not be critical of you –in fact he will appreciate you for who /what you are.

❖ A man must respect, admire, and value you. Anyone who thinks you are a doormat to be stepped on or bullied must be abandoned.

❖ A man who respects you will never try and change you or criticize you.

Think clearly, was the man who rejected you caring and considerate was he appreciative? If the answer is "No," then it is best he is out of your life.

Break ups can be agony even if the relationship is only a few days old. Whether a man or woman, whenever there is any doubt in your mind, it is best to make a clean break and not hang on to a relationship because you don't know how to say "I am sorry but this will not work."

The fact is, rejection is an essential part of the dating game. Unless, you meet the love of your life on your very first date, you'll need to meet several different suitors before you settle down.

Remember, you just cannot live life according to others you must live life for yourself and yourself only. If you set aside your needs and desires you will become an empty shell and be open to misunderstandings, unhappiness, as well as sorrow.

Believe me, you will bounce back to happiness like a rubber ball – all you need is belief in yourself.

If a person cannot love you or treat you as you are meant to be, no matter there are others who will – the world is such that there are others who will be just perfect for you.

Feel secure and confident within yourself – never feel dejected or let down.

Sharing your thoughts and feelings helps –talk about the rejection with someone close to you. Let all the feelings of hurt and resentment flush out of your system.

Move on with your life. Learn from your experience. Try and find out what went wrong—this will help you in future.

Try and answer –Why did I like him? What did I dislike? Also determine what he found likeable in you and why he decided to end the relationship.

You can prevent mistakes by being practical and analyzing things logically.

There are times in every woman's life when she may feel she is losing the battle—she is never ever going to achieve her desires and goals. It does not mean that the battle is lost but that your self-esteem has touched rock bottom and needs a boost.

There are ways in which one can raise to great levels one's self-esteem—

❖ Never compare yourself to others—this enhances negativity. You are you and Marilyn Monroe will always be herself.

❖ Never put yourself down --- never take to heart negative comments or opinions passed by others about you personally or your skills, or abilities.

❖ Negativity is like a disease – it spreads quickly and will eat you up. Everyone makes mistakes—learn from them-- don't let them pull you down.

❖ Think positively—try and see the bright side to everything. It is not hard to do-- it is a conscious effort that you must make.

❖ Be gracious and accept compliments with happiness—if you yourself decide you do not deserve them then you are headed towards a low self-esteem.

❖ Learn how to praise/acknowledge your abilities.

- ❖ Join/learn about life coaching. There are good programs, workshops, and books that will help you raise your self-esteem and develop a positive attitude.

- ❖ Mix with positive and happy/supportive people. They will never influence you or your thinking in a negative way.

- ❖ Negative people will on the other hand, try and put you down every step of the way and shoot down your decisions/ideas.

- ❖ Strong and supportive people will make you feel better about yourself and help you raise your hopes, desires, and aspirations—raise your self esteem.

- ❖ Develop a positive, loving support network.

- ❖ Acknowledge that you are not perfect. Realize that along with negative qualities you do have positive qualities as well as skills.

- ❖ Appreciate what you have, treasure it—a glass must be viewed as half full not half empty.

- ❖ Never be bullied—voice as well as acknowledge your needs. Be tolerant of others but not a doormat.

- ❖ Limit yourself to the bare essentials—you too are an individual with needs.

❖ Try and help others in small ways and large—when you do this, you will start valuing yourself more and your confidence levels will grow significantly.

❖ Involve yourself in work and activities that you love.

Life is a "funny thing" –it rewards self-help and action. If you take up a challenge, then your self-esteem rises—backing away or avoiding challenges just means that you are letting your weakness grow.

If you are secure, then you will be able to:

❖ Laugh with others and at yourself.

❖ Be proud of who you are.

❖ Have a strong sense of self.

❖ Be emotionally stable.

❖ Not fear the future and what it holds.

❖ Never be intimidated.

❖ Be comfortable and at ease in any situation.

Live life to the fullest.

Chapter 13: When it's Time to Move On

Perhaps the most difficult and hardest thing during a relationship is saying, "no." It's difficult to break off a relationship with so many emotions involved, especially the time you've shared together. Not only are you concerned about your feelings, your also concerned about his feelings...

If it has to happen, it has to happen. One cannot continue talking through email or meet a person because he is so nice...

"How do I tell him he's not my type?"

❖ **Be honest and tell the man that you liked him but don't feel any chemistry/spark.** Most men will understand. It is better to be upfront and honest than lead a man along. The longer you take the more difficult it will be. Women who lead men along are labeled as teases.

❖ **Sit down over a glass of wine or coffee** and say, "I treasure our friendship, but I don't think it can go any further than that, hope you understand."

❖ **Explain what a wonderful experience it was and that you are disappointed that there is no special feeling.** Explain that you are sure someone more suitable than you will come along.

- ❖ **Respect the person;** explain honestly why you don't think it will work. Never make it seem like it is his entire fault. Remember it takes two to form a relationship.

- ❖ **Don't drag it**, when you know you are not going anywhere with the relationship why persist. You are not doing either the man or yourself a favor the longer you hold on the more difficult it gets, so end it soon. Make a clean break.

- ❖ **Never make the mistake of overlapping**—don't start a new relationship before ending the old one. You will come across as a two-timer and not reliable.

- ❖ **Watch what you say.** Don't say, "let us be friends" it does not work. When you are considering or in a serious relationship one cannot terminate the relationship and expect to remain friends. It is not advisable at all.

- ❖ **Never break up in a public place or send him a one-line message or offline message.** It is insulting and the sign of a coward.

- ❖ **Never pick a fight or try and assign blame.** It is no way to ease personal guilt. Be open and honest. Unnecessary heartache is to be avoided.

Always state your feelings clearly don't leave any chance for doubt that things can pick up sometime or the other. A clean break is best.

Never ignore a person —always answer e-mails or messages. Silence does not mean "no" it just proves you are a rude person. Say what you feel/think honestly. Put a full stop to it and move on.

As far as dating sites are concerned you have the option of clicking "decline" if you don't want to respond to a mail sent by a member. They also provide an option where you can, by choice block mails from specific people.

If you still continue to receive unwanted mail, then shut the account down and register for a new e-mail ID. Very nasty or nuisance mails can be reported to the site – they will take the necessary steps to protect you.

One of the advantages of being online is that you don't have the emotional trauma of rejecting a person face to face—an IM or e-mail explaining why "No" can be done politely and clearly.

According to experts one must be clear in mind and heart that it is not going to work. Vacillating is unhealthy. There is either no or yes—"maybe" does not exist. Be absolutely sure before you reject a man. Secondly, never dish out the "silent treatment" – stop answering mails, ignore IMs, or refuse calls.

It is rude and disturbing. Being an ostrich is not going to help – don't hide, say what you want to clearly and in no uncertain terms. And finally, break up early in the relationship don't carry on when in doubt. It's unfair to lead a person along when you know this is not going anywhere.

Breaking up in no fun for you or the man – do it with honesty, gentleness, and compassion.

CHAPTER 14: KEEPING POSITIVE

Dating or developing a personal "relationship" is not easy at all – too many of us, it is scary and intimidating. Even if we are strong, determined, and successful in our work and daily lives when it comes to emotions or relationships most women find themselves against an insurmountable wall.

Meeting people on a personal level is scary and to take that further is terrifying. Instinctively, we don our protective and impenetrable armor.

To move ahead we must ask ourselves:

❖ How would a man or another woman perceive me?

❖ What are my positive and negative points? Do I have any shortcomings?

❖ Do I need to improve or tackle certain issues?

❖ Do I come on too strong and dominant?

❖ What are my goals as far as romance is concerned?

❖ Am I a fulfilled person?

❖ Do I only want corporate success or personal success too?

Once you jot down the answers to the above you will be able to evaluate yourself and take steps to make changes/improvements.

Each one of us must learn to weave our own magic.

❖ Determine your self-esteem —whether it is high or low. According to experts low self-esteem is created by fears of rejection and inadequacies. One must try and overcome this—be positive and set a few "joyful" goals.

❖ Have a makeover, take singing lessons, and buy a gold fish, bird, cat or dog. Adopt methods that bring joy and harmony into your life. Don't dwell on misery—misery is like a plague it grows on sympathy and moroseness. Never let negativity grow and spread like the plague.

❖ Spend time with friends who will not sympathize and make matters worse—spend time with friends who will show you the way to overcome your problems and put you on the path to successful dating.

❖ List clearly what you think your limitations are—shyness, inhibitions, introvert, feeling inadequate, berating your own looks and so on. Change what you can like a wardrobe and accept what cannot change like a hooked nose.

❖ Decide enough is enough—I am beautiful on the inside and out and there is someone out there who will appreciate me for what I am.

❖ Devise methods to build up your confidence and self-esteem---decide on what you want from life and go right ahead and achieve it.

❖ Learn to be happy—accept what went wrong and work towards making sure it does not happen again. Make goals that put you on the path to success---

➢ See the "bright" side of everything.

➢ Respect yourself –trust in your abilities, potential, and looks.

➢ Realize what your strengths are and make use of them. If you are boisterous then try not to project a sulky or sophisticated image.

➢ Accept your limitations –life will become easier if you learn to accept and make do with things as they are.

➢ Never go by what others say—only do what you are convinced about. In the end you must be happy with your decision and not do something because it is the fashionable thing to do.

❖ One can be much happier if:

❖ One is not dependant on others---a level of independent thought as well as action goes a long way.

❖ Cultivate interests that absorb you totally—do not choose a hobby because it is popular. If cooking is not "your cup of tea" do not join cooking classes take up bicycling /pot making/ theater /or trekking.

❖ All goals that you set in the field of dating must be your own and not what your friend desires or a dating advice suggests.

❖ Be honest with yourself and list down what kind of man you seek.

❖ Shyness plagues most of us except sales people—it is not an affliction to be afraid about. If one is shy and inhibited one will land up being lonely and left out—so be determined to overcome shyness. Decide mentally, I am going to smile in a friendly manner and talk about—music, weather, books, learn how to participate in a conversation by throwing in a comment or nodding your head in agreement or disagreement.

❖ If a group of colleagues/ friends are planning a trip and you want to go –say so. One does not always have to wait for an invitation –you could say "do you have room for me! Or ask may I tag along?" Very often people who are shy are mistaken as being snobbish – and that is difficult to overcome.

❖ Not all of us are style divas or Marilyn Monroe –yet the beauty within can glow giving radiance to the whole personality. Don't aim to be something you are not. Remember, not all gentlemen prefer blonds there are many who do treasure other kinds of women.

❖ Highlight your best features and only use the kind of makeup you are comfortable with---it is not essential to go with "colors or look of the season." What you wear must enhance your features not give a loud out of place appearance.

The single most important thing is to be yourself--- do not adopt behaviors that are foreign to you. Be as open and honest as you can—remember your aim is not to date and part ways but to form a successful lasting relationship. Many men appreciate honesty and openness.

Attributes that lead to a good first and lasting impression are: warmth, sense of humor, imagination, confidence, personal success, fitness, individuality, body language, conversational ability, aspirations, power, creativity, and kindness,

On the other hand, a sure fire "turn off" is:

❖ Being self-centered.

- ❖ Being closed minded and judgmental.

- ❖ Being manner less.

- ❖ Being a bad conversationalist.

- ❖ Having a negative attitude.

- ❖ Having no education.

- ❖ Being indecisive and a ditherer.

- ❖ Lacking integrity and honesty with oneself as well as others.

- ❖ Being obsessed with past relationships.

- ❖ Clinging to memories, being a whiner, having a shallow attitude.

- ❖ Being involved in manipulations and power games.

- ❖ Being dishonest in dealing with the world around you.

- ❖ Having a care-a-damn attitude and materialism.

Remember, life does not have to be dreary or come to a standstill because you are single.

The modern age brings with it its own difficulties---many of us single women are busy with careers, and many a time, social life takes a back seat. Technology may be wonderful but where social structure is concerned, it serves to make people—women and men—solitary beings.

Be it computers, cell phones, voice mail, or i-pods--- what happens in the name of faster communications is isolation. One has to make a conscious decision to set aside ambitions and technology and make time for relationships.

Practice meditation and relaxation techniques. These are sure-fire ways to keep calm, the mind free of clutter, and the soul happy. Keep an open mind and be patient. Romance does not happen in a split second; even if you did begin online dating ten weeks ago there is no need to get depressed that you have not met Mr. Right yet.

The trick is in reading profiles, sending out e-mails, responding to possible dates, and taking it from there. If things don't work at once give it some space.   Do not let finding a man become your sole purpose. You should have other aims in life, live life to the fullest, and dating or meeting Mr. Ideal should be by the by.

Try all kinds of things -- going out in groups, attending neighborhood functions, joining travel groups, volunteer organizations and more. You never know where Mr. Right will be!

Make friends with men –never view each one as "The man," if you do, you will be uncomfortable and uneasy. Just as you have other "girl" friends, men who are brothers or cousins, it is okay to have friends who are men.

One can say that it is "confidence" that makes or breaks a person. It molds the way a woman perceives life/situations, and it is what determines what action is to be taken.

What is confidence made of—it is trust. If you trust in yourself then, half the battle is won .To be confident, you need to be secure in your life, work, and environment. It is inadequacies that make a person insecure or lacking confidence.

If you are secure, then you will be able to:

❖ Laugh with others and at yourself.

❖ Be proud of who you are.

❖ Have a strong sense of self.

❖ Be emotionally stable.

❖ Not fear the future and what is holds.

❖ Never be intimidated.

❖ Be comfortable and at ease in any situation.

To date successfully, a woman needs to understand her confidence levels. Some things can be changed quickly while others will be done over time and with concerted effort. The crux is to try and not think—"what's the point—I am a failure anyway."

Start by:

- ❖ Making a list of your positive traits and negative traits. Ask a friend to check them through. Then begin to work out the kinks.

- ❖ Review how you look and dress—work on this aspect first as it is the easiest to change. Be comfortable with any changes you make—don't put streaks in your hair if they make you uncomfortable even if they are in fashion.

- ❖ Ensure you are in shape—a fitness regime does wonders for the mind and body.

- ❖ Make changes in routines that make you feel lousy--- if meeting X, Y, and Z makes you feel like a louse then stop meeting them. Weed out all relationships /actions that undermine your self-esteem/confidence.

- ❖ Decide—I am going to live life to the fullest. Take courage and do things you have always dreamt of –even if it's a candle business or *pranic* healing.

- ❖ Make priority one –yourself.

❖ Widen your horizons. Explore the world outside your immediate circle.

❖ Be selective about who you meet/cultivate. Avoid people who make fun of you or put you down constantly.

❖ Go out on dates — assuming the date is a friend you are going to meet. This way, there will be no underlying sexual tension.

❖ There must be more to life than love and dating — set a few life goals.

❖ Be confident enough to ask someone you like out— there is nothing wrong with that.

❖ Walk away instantly from anything that makes you sad /upset /or nervy

❖ The more the people you meet, the happier you will be.

There are a few key factors:

❖ State of mind.

❖ Physical appearance.

❖ Style.

❖ Listening skills.

❖ Volatility.

❖ Experience.

❖ Finance.

If you are aspiring to be a person who is 100% confident then you must incorporate, monitor, adapt, imbibe, and balance all the above characteristics. What forms the foundation is, of course, "a belief in yourself."

Where women are concerned, what is most essential is inner confidence—confident women are seen as being "sexy".

❖ Learn to be confident—believe in yourself and set aside insecurities.

❖ Speak with conviction and walk tall.

❖ Try not to be afraid of life—there are no monsters except in our own minds. If you have any doubts/ problems talk to someone—a family member, close friend, or counselor.

❖ Feel good inside and out—look and act confident. You will find that people respond to you quite differently. Stand tall have a wonderful posture even if you are just 4 feet tall —hold your head high with your shoulders straight, place your feet about a foot apart this will give you a well balanced stance.

❖ Maintain eye contact with people—if you look down or away it conveys insecurities.

- Exude happiness—a positive expression will do wonders as will a smile. Make your self-approachable instead of cold and distant.

- Work out nervous habits—they signal lack of confidence. Fidgeting with hands, nodding you head incessantly, twirling your hair, playing with the clasp of your bag, are all "No No" actions.

- Mentally jot down what you normally do while speaking to, or dinning with others of the opposite sex and, consciously work towards improving yourself or refining your attitudes.

- Never try and disappear into the woodwork—make a place for yourself in life.

- Speak out—try and participate in conversations/activities. This does not mean becoming greedy and holding center stage.

Most relationships that are successful generally have a confident, self-assured woman in it. It is important to realize, that a relationship is never going to fill a lacuna in you. It is up to you to have a busy schedule and many interests —one of which should be dating.

To be loved, one must first love oneself. Giving to a partner and receiving strengthens a relationship—it will make you feel needed and loved. If you feel your confidence being undermined or you begin to feel disrespect / lowly—then the relationship is not for you --walk away before it gets serious. Any relationship should be a two way street –not give give, give.

If you are just healing from a broken relationship then give your self-space and time—time is a great healer. Do not jump into another relationship—on the rebound it will never work. Sympathy should never be mistaken for love. Give yourself three months to a year before you get back into dating—it gives you time to "get over things."

❖ If you need something from a man ask for it ---men welcome confident requests. Never hint or beat about the bush.

❖ Show you care don't be inhibited—cuddle, hug, kiss, and more.

❖ It's okay to refuse a request that you are uncomfortable with—men will respect you for it.

❖ Try and set yourself new goals/challenges. Accomplishing challenges will keep fear and inadequacies at bay. Celebrate when you have achieved even a small goal – remember it's your victory however small.

The purpose of dating is to find someone we can live with in harmony and joy. It is about fulfillment in many ways—of the mind, body, as well as soul. And, dating is a means of gaining a realistic idea of Mr. Right.

The "magical key" is positivity --- it helps everyone conquer their fears and doubts. Surround yourself with happy contended people.

Misery multiplies quickly and is a dreadful disease. Avoid people who are gossips, miserable, and negative. Let both your mind and soul be free of shackles.

Happiness always stems from within and you will find that different people have different paths to tread. Accept life and all it has to offer with both hands. Remember, one can either be a part of the world, or hide away from it.

Join the moving stream of life take the "plus and minuses" in your stride –and you will succeed.

Reaching a personal goal will bring about a sense of fulfillment and confidence. Once you have conquered your inner self, help others to do so. A friendly world is a happy world.

Fear and insecurities are there throughout our lives -- they never go away but once we learn that they can be conquered, life becomes bearable and one can look forward to happiness. Music, singing, gardening, and so on work magic and dispel all negativity and introduce joyous happiness—practice one hobby that you like.

Today a person you meet may be a stranger but tomorrow, he/she will become a friend, loved one, and a partner for life.

Grab life and all it has to offer with both hands.

Chapter 15: Online Safety Concerns

With the anonymity of online dating, one must be really aware of the risks involved with meeting a total stranger. Use precaution when meeting someone new and never get carried away. Use good judgment and be cautious of the individuals you meet.

Here are a few key safety tips to keep in mind:

❖ **Do not believe everything you read online.** People tend to lie about their age, size, children, occupation and more. Be cautious and try and vet a person you like as much as possible. Humans have a natural tendency to create fantasies.

❖ **Never reveal your personal details**—addresses, workplace address, phone numbers, banking details and so on. Always set up a separate e-mail account for online dating or use the anonymity provided by the sites. It is safer or you will be placing yourself in danger.

❖ **Try not to jump the gun and rush into a relationship.** Be tough and contain your enthusiasm—even if he is perfect, he can wait until you are sure. Look out for inconsistencies in answers to questions, or if a person is hiding facts about himself. Don't be blinded by the concept of being in love.

❖ **Ensure cyber safety**—read about it and be sure to implement it. Even when you decide to speak on the phone never give your personal numbers to anyone –even if you feel they are dependable.

❖ **If you are uncomfortable or being troubled by anyone online report them to the dating site.** Immediately close your e-mail ids and avoid going online for a few days. Try and protect yourself as best as possible.

❖ **Look out for members who use inappropriate language or photographs.**

❖ **Avoid anyone who is intimidating or threatening.**

❖ **Watch out for duplicity.**

❖ **Be vigilant** about any man who displays: anger, frustrations, domination, controlling behaviors, obsessions and so on. Read about such traits and why they are not suitable in a man you want to date.

❖ **When you decide to meet in person do so in a public place**; take a friend along; always leave a note for the family stating where you are going and with whom; arrange for a family member or friend to call you during your date; it is safer to have your own transportation; never allow a stranger into your home.

Before joining any dating site ensure:

❖ They have a privacy policy in place.

❖ That the code of ethics of the site is in place.

❖ The terms and conditions are such that they take action against inappropriate/criminal behavior.

❖ That they have standards for language as well as photographs—vulgarity is not acceptable.

❖ Their customer service and support is the best in the industry.

Safety concerns /guidelines are for your own good—know about them and be sure to practice them. Avoid large chat rooms and ones that do not have any rules or monitoring.

Red Flags must always be kept in mind. It is for your own protection.

❖ **Look out for warning signs** like displays of: anger, extreme frustration, attempts to pressurize you, a controlling nature, aggressiveness, whining nature. Be wary of men who make demeaning or disrespectful comments.

❖ **Avoid liars**—those who provide inconsistent information of age, interests, appearance, marital status, profession, financial status and so on.

- ❖ **Beware of men who blow hot and cold**—establish online contact and then avoid phone calls or hedge.

- ❖ **Be vigilant** of those who avoid answering questions or do not give direct answers.

- ❖ **Watch out for men whose online persona is at variance from his actual persona.**

- ❖ **Never trust men who avoid introducing you to friends**, colleagues, family members—who try and hide their relationship to you. Those who pretend you don't exist if they meet someone they know when they are with you.

- ❖ **Question any man who posts an outdated photograph** or a photo of someone else.

- ❖ **He is not clear about why he states separated as status**— is unwilling to give details.

- ❖ **He is obsessed with the physical attributes of women**— and keep emphasizing that, watch out he may be just trying for casual sex.

- ❖ **Men who state that they seek a discrete relationship**—is probably cheating on his wife.

- ❖ **Talks about sex without even knowing you**—seems obsessed by it.

- ❖ **Tries to get personal details too soon and too anxiously**--- could be a stalker.

- ❖ **A man who is difficult to get on the phone** and if you ring him randomly you can hear female voices in the background—the man may be in a relationship and looking for more.

- ❖ **A man who asks for financial help** or seeks information about money. Or offers to invest on your behalf.

- ❖ **Is too anxious to know about your wealth** and possessions.

- ❖ **Shows signs of insecurity**, loneliness, resentment towards others, or rejection. Such men will be difficult and hard to be happy with—they will squeeze you for their own emotional security.

- ❖ **Men who are self obsessed**—think of themselves only and not of others. Hard to live with as they will show no consideration or respect for women.

Be sensible and realistic—don't expect to meet prince charming on the very first day. For every perfect man there will be hundreds of imperfect ones. Look for compatibility not to being swept off your feet.

Before you start making contact consider geography – are you prepared to fly out to meet Mr. X -- is it realistic to begin a long distance friendship/relationship? Think, what are my limitations? How far am I prepared to go? Believe me, common sense and instincts can be your two greatest allies.

Always keep your wits and instincts about you. Never float on a cloud—dreams can quickly turn into nightmares. Be sexually responsible and never agree to anything you are not sure about or comfortable with.

Dating is not a risk-free zone—a little bit of vigilance can prevent heartache.

Final Thoughts

Life is passing by ever so quickly, but even then, love should not be rushed. It should be savored and enjoyed each moment you experience it. Remember to let your heart do the feeling and the mind do the thinking. Keep your eyes and ears open, and use careful judgment when choosing your Mr. Right. Take the time and effort to understand what you really want and also what you are looking for. And remember, you're in control of who you want to date.

As mentioned before, online dating is real, it's not a fad. Individuals today are taking advantage of this wonderful opportunity of online dating and many are becoming successful with it. Dating online should is not a monster to be feared. It offers a chance to seek and find your ideal man.

Dating online presents, infallible ways of meeting, understanding, and knowing a man, what he seeks in a partner, and whether you and the man have anything in common. There is no awkwardness or embarrassment

However proceed with extra caution and knowledge.

Keep your eyes open and heart free. Dare to dream and your dreams will come true!

****